TOP TEN BRO-JITSU MOVES

1. Stop Hitting Yourself
2. Hanging Spit Fake
3. Wedgie
4. Full-Body Defensive Fish Wiggle
5. Nipple Cripple
6. Wet Willy
7. Preemptive Cry of Pain
8. Two for Flinching
9. Dogpile
10. Pink Belly

These moves will *save your life.*

BRO-JITSU

THE MARTIAL ART OF *SIBLING SMACKDOWN*

Daniel H. Wilson, PhD
illustrated by Les McClaine

BLOOMSBURY

NEW YORK BERLIN LONDON

Like all serious martial arts, Bro-Jitsu should be practiced with caution. The author and publisher are not responsible for any injury— mental, physical, or imaginary—that may result from the use of these techniques.

Text copyright © 2010 by Daniel H. Wilson
Illustrations copyright © 2010 by Les McClaine
All rights reserved. No part of this book may be used or reproduced in any manner whatsoever without written permission from the publisher, except in the case of brief quotations embodied in critical articles or reviews.

Published by Bloomsbury Books for Young Readers
175 Fifth Avenue, New York, New York 10010

Library of Congress Cataloging-in-Publication Data
Wilson, Daniel H. (Daniel Howard).
Bro-Jitsu : the martial art of sibling smackdown / Daniel H. Wilson;
illustrated by Les McClaine. — 1st U.S. ed.
p.   cm.
Includes index.
ISBN-13: 978-1-59990-279-1 • ISBN-10: 1-59990-279-6
1. Martial arts—Humor. 2. Sibling rivalry—Humor. 3. Brothers and sisters—Humor.
I. McClaine, Les, ill. II. Title. III. Title: Martial art of sibling smackdown.
PN6231.M325W55 2009   306.87502'07—dc22   2008030308

Art created digitally
Typeset in New York to Las Vegas, Chinese Takeout, and Aaux
Book design by Yelena Safronova

First U.S. Edition April 2010
Printed in China by South China Printing Company, Dongguan City, Guangdong
2 4 6 8 10 9 7 5 3 1

All papers used by Bloomsbury U.S.A. are natural, recyclable products made from wood grown in well-managed forests. The manufacturing processes conform to the environmental regulations of the country of origin.

For my little brother

CONTENTS

INTRODUCTION

Welcome to the first and only guide to Bro-Jitsu—the world's most ancient and powerful martial art. Bro-Jitsu is a highly stylized form of physical and mental combat whose origins are lost to time; it has been practiced and honed to perfection over countless millennia by billions of human beings who all share one crucial thing in common: annoying siblings.

In the last few decades, the role between adults and children has evolved to become more safe, more positive, and much more politically correct. The days of getting a paddling at school are over, and the days of wobbling oversize helmets and excessive padding have arrived. The world may be nicer, but children haven't changed. Empires will rise and fall, social conventions will come and go, but learning to burp into your brother's face just as he inhales is a skill that will never lose its intrinsic value.

It is this universal, ageless quality of Bro-Jitsu that makes it a mandatory martial art for anyone who has one or more siblings. Age, gender, and physical condition have no bearing whatsoever on your ultimate ability to reach the fabled level of Bro-master. As long as you have brothers, sisters, cousins, or childhood friends—Bro-Jitsu is the inescapable way of life laid before you.

Although participation is mandatory, truly understanding and mastering Bro-Jitsu has serious benefits. The simple fact is that to properly form a lifelong bond of brother- or sisterhood, human beings must aggravate each other, push each other around, and bother the heck out of each other. Otherwise, brothers and sisters might as well be polite strangers on the bus. The unique enduring love-hate relationship between siblings is why Bro-Jitsu is the single most practiced martial art ever put into use by humankind (and to a lesser extent, monkeykind).

This book breaks down the martial art of Bro-Jitsu into three strategies: offensive moves, defensive moves, and psychological moves. Each section will deliver step-by-step instructions on performing crucial techniques, as well as handy countermoves and additional variations suitable for more advanced students. These techniques are intended for use by sibling combatants, while any nearby parents naturally fulfill the role of parental referees. Parents are duty-bound to interfere with Bro-Jitsu bouts but should be considered roadblocks that must be coaxed, goaded, and fooled by wily children who intend to excel in their study of Bro-Jitsu. Throughout the course of this book, readers will learn to attack, defend, and manipulate their way through thousands of battles in an ongoing war of Bro-Jitsu that will last for as long as there are siblings.

You, honorable reader, sit on the precipice of greatness. Now is the time to ask yourself: do I have the courage and determination—the sheer grit and force of will—to master Bro-Jitsu?

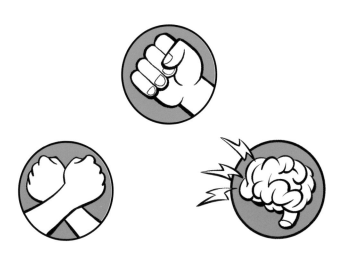

WARNING: DEALING WITH ONLY CHILDREN

A percentage of people on this planet do not have siblings. Scientists call these unfortunate people "only children." These only children can be found anywhere; they may be people you play with or people you ride the bus to school with. Be careful. Without years of daily training in Bro-Jitsu, only children may never properly learn how to tease, taunt, or rassle. An only child may take casual insults to heart. After a friendly *noogie*, *headlock*, or *wet willy*, an only child may react by punching you in the face, causing real blood to come out of your nose or lip. Stay alert and do not be taken by surprise: an only child can be as dangerous as a cornered badger.

THE CODE OF BRO-JITSU

Bro-Jitsu is a proud martial art with a long and glorious tradition. Walking the path of Bro-Jitsu will not be easy. Only those with strength, intelligence, and steaming gobs of self-discipline will successfully make the transition from snot-nosed sibling into calm Bro-Jitsu master.

Respect, courtesy, and honor. None of these are necessary qualities for a beginning student of Bro-Jitsu. Younger siblings must instead focus on other qualities, such as being irritating, selfish, and loud. On the other hand, older siblings should develop body- and soul-crushing physical attacks, the ability to tell young children outlandish lies with a straight face, and the ultimate Bro-power of the *strong ignore*. Always remember: the purpose of Bro-Jitsu is to defeat your siblings, not to improve yourself. Trust me, you're just fine. Your evil brothers and sisters, however, must be physically pummeled and mentally tricked so that you may live to see another day and so that you can watch your favorite TV show without having the remote stolen.

An accomplished student of Bro-Jitsu will know and understand that others may stray from the path and shatter the sacred code of Bro-Jitsu. Enraged little sisters, coldhearted parents, or clueless only children—any of these foes may soil the field of sibling combat with illegal or unfair moves. Condition yourself to follow the code in the face of cheaters and neophytes; it will not only make you a better person, but a better brother or sister.

Ultimately, Bro-Jitsu is about family. Friends and sweethearts may come and go, but your siblings are going to stick around for the rest of your life. This is the great and paradoxical reward for a lifetime of proper Bro-Jitsu: via countless cheap shots, scathing jibes, and the blackest artifice, you will gradually form a sacred bond of deep trust with and grudging respect from your brothers and sisters. Nothing can break this bond, which has been forged in the crucible of childhood and tempered with the joys and tears of innumerable Bro-Jitsu battles.

While many of the techniques in this book may visually resemble techniques from other schools of martial art—such as karate, aikido, and no-holds-barred pro wrestling—their execution is radically different in the realm of Bro-Jitsu. Unless the instructions and accompanying illustrations are followed carefully, the beginning student will only duplicate the moves through physical force and will fail to follow the true code of Bro-Jitsu, which is a combination of body and spirit.

As we grow into adults, the age differences between siblings evaporate, our most traumatic memories take on the happy glow of childhood, and our parents may actually even become our friends (although they remain referees as well). If the path of Bro-Jitsu has been followed, you will come to realize that the siblings whom you have struggled against for years have become your greatest allies and most trusted comrades. When that time comes, enjoy the relationship you have with your brothers and sisters—you've undoubtedly earned it.

SACRED VOW OF BRO-JITSU

It is crucial to understand and acknowledge the underlying code of honor that guides your journey into the martial art of sibling rivalry. The following sacred vow encapsulates the heart and soul of Bro-Jitsu. As you repeat these words out loud (preferably in the bathroom with the door locked), be mindful that this is a vow to yourself, your family, and to the generations of brave Bro-Jitsu warriors who came before you.

Once made, this vow should never be broken. Or at least, not very often.

✦ I promise I will never hit my sibling in the face, even if (s)he always breaks my stuff and gets away with it, too.

✦ I will strive to physically and mentally torture my siblings to make them stronger, better people. But I will do my best to never injure or scar them permanently.

I will never team up with outsiders against my sibling because we are joined by an unbreakable bond of kinship. Plus, I will be in a lot of trouble with Mom if anything ever happens to my sibling.

I will continue to refine and improve the techniques of Bro-Jitsu long after reaching adulthood so that my siblings will never grow soft—and so that they will never forget how freaking awesome I am and how much they totally suck.

AUTHOR'S NOTE

*T*he terminology used to describe martial arts moves differs from one school to the next. To avoid confusion, I have chosen to use the terms commonly employed by children of the North American variety. Alternate terms for moves are included when appropriate. The participants in Bro-Jitsu are generally referred to as *attackers* and *defenders*, although they may also be referred to as *siblings*, *opponents*, or *victims*. Due to the role they usually play, parents are referred to as *parental referees*. In moves that require examples, gender has been chosen randomly to illustrate the point at hand. Unless specifically stated, every Bro-Jitsu move could (and should) be applied to siblings of any age or gender.

OFFENSIVE MOVES

The spiritual bond of sibling kinship will never be strong if siblings' bodies are weak. With this philosophy in mind, a set of special offensive moves have evolved over the ages that are designed to try the patience, pain thresholds, and physical stamina of children around the world. Most brothers and sisters may not realize it, but wrestling, jostling, and sticking fingers into each other's ears are part of a crucial training regimen that leads to strong bones, muscles . . . and eardrums.

In this chapter, we explore a set of Bro-Jitsu moves that are offensive in every sense of the word. These bold moves rest on a sturdy foundation of physical strength and draw deeply from an arsenal of disgusting bodily functions, such as burping, farting, and spitting. Properly applied, Bro-fensive techniques can be tailored and leveraged to cause anything from mild irritation to nuclear war. Think carefully before applying the more devastating brute-force attacks in Bro-Jitsu combat.

Use the Basics

Certain Bro-Jitsu moves come so naturally that it may seem absurd to even describe them. On the contrary, these moves require the most careful description of all, because they will be used over and over again in nearly any fighting situation. Learn these moves well; you're likely going to use them every single day of your childhood (and then later in life at holidays, graduations, and weddings).

Bite

Open your mouth wide, get your tongue out of the way, and then sink your teeth into a fleshy part of your sibling, such as the forearm, calf, or pinky finger. This move is not recommended for regular use—like many great Bro-Jitsu moves, biting is completely unsanitary, but unlike other brilliant moves, biting is also likely to leave a mark that will plant blame squarely on the biter.

Caution: This move is often a little sister's last line of defense. Be wary, as a cornered sister can quickly turn into a biter.

Variations:
Snatch the Cricket

A truly skilled (or dangerously bored) Bro-Jitsuer can play this game, in which one sibling sticks out her finger and tries to put it into her brother's mouth before his jaw snaps down on it.

Teeth Snap

As an alternative to viciously mauling your siblings, consider using your toothy bite as a deterrent only. Bare your fangs threateningly and snap your teeth. (The best Bro-Jitsu moves are shared between all higher primates, including humans.) This move is guaranteed to keep your siblings' fingers out of your face and away from your french fries, but make sure an enterprising sib doesn't toss a quarter or a piece of chewed gum into your open mouth.

Hair Pull

Grab a handful of hair and give it a sharp yank. To inflict maximum pain, grab hair at the base of the neck and pull straight up, against the grain.

This staple move is quick, leaves no mark, and will always get an immediate reaction from your sibling.

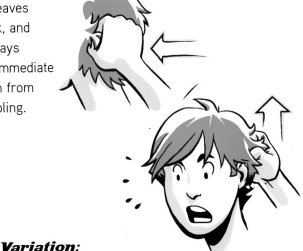

Variation:
Delayed Hair Pull

Heighten your enjoyment and increase the surprise of a classic *hair pull* by building in a delay mechanism. For example, step on your sister's hair while she's lying on the floor watching TV and wait patiently. Or roll your sister's hair up in the car window while she is asleep. When she wakes up and tries to move, you will experience the hilarious satisfaction of a job well done.

Kick

The basic kick is a staple of any Bro-Jitsu battle, whether it is used as an offensive or defensive move. To wreak havoc with your legs, follow these instructions: stand up, balance on one foot, lift your other foot into the air, and drive it into your sibling with all your might. If you've got the balance, keep your foot in the air and go back for seconds with another solid kick.

Variations:
Feets of Strength

Both siblings sit on opposite sides of the couch with their feet meeting in the center, knees bent slightly. The first one who can extend his or her legs over the whole couch (ideally crushing his opponent in the process) will win. If you're quick enough, you can shove your opponent's knees right into her own face. The winner earns the right to lie on the couch, and depending on the rules, may be allowed to rest his feet on the defeated opponent.

Stealth Butt Kick

While walking side by side, shift the weight off the leg that is away from your sibling and bend your knee. Now deliver a quick behind-the-back *kick* to the seat of your sibling's pants and keep walking. If blamed for the kick, deny it. If kicked back, *tell* Mom.

Terminator

While sharing a couch, brace your back against one arm and place both of your feet on your sibling's torso. Pushing back against the couch, use your legs to squeeze your sibling against the other arm of the couch. Slowly increase the pressure until your sibling is grunting for help, unconscious, or able to wiggle free.

Countermove:
Shin Bash

Just as your sibling raises a leg to kick, extend your foot swiftly at his shin level. The attacker will only get hurt if he chooses to drive his shin into the bottom of your waiting foot.

Punch

This old-fashioned favorite never goes out of style. Curl your fingers into a fist—thumb wrapped around your fingers—and take a swing at your sib. (If you place your thumb on the inside, you might break it.) Whether throwing a wild roundhouse or repeatedly jabbing, a good solid punch will get the job done. Just remember: never in the face.

Variations:
Dead Arm (aka Frog)

A true Bro-master will never throw a *punch* without a specific target in mind. By targeting the perfect spot of the opponent's upper shoulder or upper thigh, a single *punch* can paralyze an entire arm or leg for several minutes. This approach inflicts maximum pain in a single blow, which is crucial when only a few *punches* will be landed (e.g., when nailing somebody *two for flinching*).

Not My Fault

Pretend you're a robot and mechanically punch the air. While maintaining this steady punching motion, walk toward your sibling and stop just out of range. Viciously punch the air where your sibling wants to go. Now whose fault is it if she walks into your furious fists? Not yours, my friend. Not yours.

Sucker Punch

Sometimes it is impossible to penetrate the defenses of a prepared sibling. In these situations, distract your sibling by pointing at a UFO or feigning a life-threatening injury. The second that his guard is down, deliver a fierce *punch* to the stomach. And don't forget the most important step of a sucker punch—run!

Shoulder Pin

Siblings will rarely stay still while the most humiliating Bro-Jitsu moves are being dealt out, and so their pesky arms must first be secured. By far the most common approach is to pin your sibling on her back with your knees on her shoulders. First, use a *trip* to position your sibling on the ground. Next, climb onto her chest and pin her arms down with your knees. You're now free to transition into a variety of other attacks, from a simple *tickle* to the dreaded *hanging spit fake*. Use your imagination and just have fun with it, you know?

Countermove:
Knee to the Back

It can be an awful experience to be helplessly pinned down by your sibling. To escape, jerk your knee up and jab your attacker in the back. If you have the flexibility, lift your foot up and kick the attacker in the back of the head. You will probably only get one shot before the attacker changes position, so make it count!

Wrist Grab

Since it isn't always convenient to tackle your sib to the ground for a *shoulder pin*, the wrist grab is a common method for humiliation on the go. As long as you are the bigger and stronger sibling, just grab your brother or sister by the wrists and then transfer both wrists to one of your hands. Now you have one hand free to do, like, whatever.

Variation:
Sleeve Grab

In the wintertime it's a cinch to secure your sibling's hands and arms as long as he is wearing
long sleeves. Yank down one sleeve past your
sibling's hand and hold it tight. With one of his
arms now secured, it will be even easier to do
the same thing with the other sleeve. Now hold
both sleeves closed with one hand and torture
away with your free hand. Alternately, tie the
sleeves together in a knot and dedicate both
hands to the task of humiliating your brother.

Living Room Warfare

Every martial art has a traditional arena in which formal contests are held. In karate, it is a dojo. Bro-Jitsu is commonly performed in the living room, sometimes called "the den" or "family room." The living room is home to safe, padded surfaces like couches and chairs, as well as jagged chin busters such as coffee tables and magazine racks. It also contains many of the greatest resources of the home, including comfortable seats, video-game consoles, and, of course, the television. It is in this unpredictable environment that your skills and abilities will be honed and your fate decided.

Butt Busters

Stuff as many pillows as you can fit into the seat of your baggy sweatpants. Face off at opposite ends of the living room and do your best to intimidate the enemy for a few seconds. Now sprint toward each other like a couple of padded rhinos, spin at the last instant, and plow into a collision of well-protected behinds.

Note: This move requires the cooperation of both siblings. Resist the urge to jump out of the way just as your sister leaps at you backward.

Variation:
Belly Buster

Alternately, stuff your shirt with pillows, pick up one couch cushion each, and clash like a couple of mini sumo wrestlers. Just try not to accidentally head-butt your sister.

Couch Fort

The traditional defensive structure of Bro-Jitsu is built of the thick, impact-absorbent cushions located on the family couch. Although designs can be arbitrarily complicated, the basic couch fort is composed of three cushions—two walls and a ceiling. (The back and arms of the couch can serve as extra walls.) Blankets should

be placed atop couch forts to create more security. Additional pillows may be used as ammunition in pillow fights or as decorative architectural features.

Note: Hide-A-Bed couches have a secret cavity underneath that can be used as a last-ditch hiding place during a Bro-Jitsu catastrophe.

Variation: Indoor Tent

The indoor tent is less sturdy than a *couch fort*, but can be built in more locations and can serve as a crucial fallback point when parental referees reclaim the couch to watch television. Collect a large top sheet and clothespins from the laundry room. Bungee cords, twine, and duct tape also work but are generally frowned upon by parental referees. Using clothespins, secure the sheet from chairs, tables, and doorknobs to create a ceiling and walls for your tent. (Depending on the climate, consider hanging one end of the sheet over the air conditioner or heater.) Now layer the floor with blankets, haul in comic books and refreshments, and start your rugged campout.

Note: Choose your sheet carefully—a neutral pattern will work for anyone, while vintage New Kids on the Block sheets are not advised under any circumstance.

Own the Remote Control

The holy grail of the living room goes by many names: "the remote," "the clicker," or in more literal families, simply "the box." Regardless of what you call it, this device controls the TV and as we all know—he who controls the television, controls the living room. Several strategic variations exist for securing the remote:

Variations:
Batteries Not Included

Find the remote control, turn it to the desired channel, and then remove and hide the batteries. Now the Bro-Jitsu battle is one step removed from the remote, which means you'll be more likely to watch your show during the ensuing fight over the batteries. That's okay—every minute counts.

B.Y.O.R.

That's right, bring your own remote. Universal remote controls are cheap to purchase and can be programmed to work with almost any television. If existing remotes are hidden or stripped of batteries, use your own remote to take over. Just don't let it fall into enemy hands.

Mutually Assured Destruction

Locate the small reddish square of plastic on the front of your television. This is the infrared (IR) receiver that accepts commands from the remote control. Cover this window with a piece of black electrical tape (or any other opaque object) so that no remote controls will work, period. Now change the channels the old-fashioned way by using the buttons on the TV and stay close to the television to guard against interference.

Pillow Fight

Like a postapocalyptic Thunderdome, the living room comes equipped with its own weapons—they're called "pillows." Also found in bedrooms, these padded devices come in many shapes and sizes that make them perfect for a variety of offensive maneuvers.

Variations:
Club Pillow

The main form of pillow offense is your good old bedroom pillow, the lumpier the better. Before battle, reach into the pillowcase and double over the pillow inside so that it forms a solid lump. Now wrap the open end of the pillowcase around your fist and prepare to dish out some serious pillow punishment by swinging your new "club."

Note: Filling the pillowcase with metal Hot Wheels cars is uncalled for.

Shield Pillow

Big square pillows need love, too. In fact, they are perfectly suited as defensive shields. Use one in your off hand to block an incoming blow before you take a retaliatory swing, or throw one into your sibling's face just before you beat him into submission with your mighty *club pillow*.

The Smother Brother

Find the biggest pillows in the room (and you'd better believe that includes couch cushions) and toss them en masse on top of your sibling. Once the defender is buried like an earthquake victim, do a running belly flop on top of the pile—just to make your point.

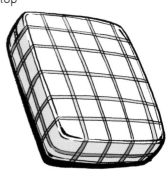

Throw Pillow

Anyone who lives with a mother will notice small, useless pillows littered all around the house (but concentrated in the living room). These are called "throw pillows" and that is exactly what they are for. Choose small, square throw pillows and ignore pillows bearing embroidered Scottie dogs or inspirational sayings, such as "If you don't believe in angels, then you haven't met my grandmother."

Caution: Throw the pillow like a ninja throwing star, but watch out for tassels and zippers—they can really sting!

Countermove: The Last Starfighter

As a desperation move when all seems lost, choose the smallest pillows in the room and toss them into the ceiling fan. The mechanical device spinning overhead will shoot your padded missiles in random directions, just like the "starburst" maneuver employed in the movie *The Last Starfighter*.

Place Back!

It is a scientific rule that there is only a single desirable place to sit in any given living room—even if multiple seats are exactly identical. Knowing this, it can be difficult to leave a coveted spot unprotected just to answer the call of nature, or the telephone. By yelling out the words "Place back!" or "Seat back!" immediately after rising, you invoke the sacred code of Bro-Jitsu, demanding that your seat be waiting for you when you return.

Note: Over time, this move may evolve to include sayings like "Box back!" or "Microwave corndog back!" or "Everything back when I get back!"

Make Them Ask for It

Bro-Jitsu is a seriously psychological martial art and many of its most offensive moves reflect that. Rather than simply attacking your sibling with overwhelming force, the rules of Bro-Jitsu call for a series of mind games first. A Bro-master will both physically and mentally dominate his or her siblings, and that means not only beating them up, but making them ask for it.

Exit Control

By far the most tiresome part of picking on your sibling is all the frantic chasing. Instead, why not lure her to you, like the deadly Venus flytrap, by carefully setting up situations in which your sibling needs to get somewhere, but you're blocking the way? For example, put on your football pads, throw your sister's favorite doll into the yard and turn on the sprinklers, then block the back door. Also, always be sure to place yourself in a good defensive position. For instance, grab your brother's video-game controller and climb to the top of your bunk bed armed with a Wiffle ball bat.

Hurts, Donut?

Innocently ask your sibling if she would like a donut. If your sibling is wary of your motive, slyly remove her suspicions by holding out a delicious, pink-frosted donut. If your poor, naive sibling actually says yes, immediately deliver a *punch* and then ask, "Hurts, don't it?" When you see disappointment mingled with pain spread across your sibling's face, you'll know that you have executed this move correctly. Reward yourself immediately with a delicious donut.

Loser Says What?

This tactic heads the long list of Bro-Jitsu moves that will only work successfully once or twice. Quickly mutter the above line and then wait for your brother to ask "What?" When and if he does, it's your obligation to let him know that he has personally confirmed what you long suspected—that he's a big loser. Share this fact with any friends and family who may be nearby.

Okay?

This game takes a more subtle approach to pain infliction. While your sibling is not paying attention, touch your index finger and thumb together to make an "Okay" hand signal. Place the circle someplace noticeable, like on your chest. If your sibling looks at this "circle of death," he has visually consented to a *punch*. (The blow must be delivered with the other hand while keeping the

circle intact.) Over time, this game will teach siblings to maintain a broad awareness while consciously focusing their attention on one spot.

Countermove:
Break the Circle

If you've accidentally looked at the "Okay" gesture (again), the ensuing blows can be averted by breaking the ring with your finger. Using one hand to hold off the attack, reach over with the other and yank the "Okay" circle apart.

Two for Flinching

An unwritten rule exists between all siblings: if you show weakness, expect to be punished. Over the years, continued use of this move will create strong, fearless siblings who won't back down, no matter what. To use this move, make a violent gesture toward your sibling (e.g., rush over while screaming with your fists out), but stop just short of touching. If she flinches, or cringes away from the blow, you may legally announce "two for flinching" and then deliver two *punches* to the upper arm.

Incorporate Professional Wrestling Moves

Everyone knows that professional wrestling is fake—well, mostly. Although the winners may be chosen beforehand, there is no denying that those brawny, oiled-up, histrionic musclemen (and -women) really do throw each other around the ring like rag dolls. The impulse to put these dazzling moves to use on your brothers and sisters is inescapable, so find a wide-open space and put these modified Bro-wrestling moves to good use. Oiling up is optional.

Bear Hug

This crushing sternum grip can be used by older brothers and sisters to subdue squirrelly younger siblings. While facing your sibling, wrap both your arms around her and channel all of your ferocious love into a grinding squeeze.

Caution: A pale face means "go," a red face means "slow down," and a blue face means "somebody call 911!"

Body Press

As a big sibling, it can be difficult to torture your younger, smaller siblings without accidentally going too far and over-torturing them. The body press is a useful move for delivering bone-crushing pain in strictly measured

amounts. Assume a push-up stance over your supine sib—body raised on palms and toes, legs slightly apart, and arms spread at a comfortable distance. Now bend your elbows and lower your bulk onto a trapped sibling. Once he is wheezing or begging for mercy, lift yourself up so your sibling can get a breath. Now repeat.

Variations:
"What if I Died Like This?"

During a *body press*, ask this question and then collapse with all of your dead weight trapping your little sister underneath. As she struggles to push you off (and breathe), go completely rigid and mention regretfully that "rigor mortis must be setting in."

Heart Attack!

Alternately, clutch your chest and fall down flopping. As you spaz out all over your little brother and crush him under your weight, be sure to innocently plead for him to call an ambulance or to "Go find my heart pills!"

Body Slam

This famous move requires significant strength or a very tiny sibling. It differs from pro wrestling in that it also requires a fluffy couch. Grab your sibling by the chest and crotch, lift him as high into the air as possible, and turn in place several times until the crowd is roaring for blood. Now toss the defender onto the couch like a sack of potatoes. Repeat until your arms are too tired to continue (or you miss the couch).

Headlock

This move is a great starting point for many other maneuvers. Position yourself behind the defender. Reach one arm around the defender's shoulders and wrap it around his head. Now pull the head down and wrap your forearm beneath the neck. Latch your hands together and squeeze to your heart's delight.

Variation:
Reverse Headlock

This move puts your sibling's head facing backward, allowing access to her ribs. Shove the defender's head into your armpit and then execute the regular headlock maneuver.

Python Leg Squeeze

This is a subjugation move that can be used to end an ongoing fight. For example, use it after a long irritating day of shopping for school clothes with your siblings. Wrap your legs around the defender's waist and lock your heels. Now flex your thighs and watch your sibling turn red and her eyes pop out. Occasionally, loosen your grip so that the defender can breathe, but lock tightly if she tries to speak—the grunting is hysterical.

Spread Eagle

Like all wrestling-inspired moves, this is a fun-to-perform and potentially lethal maneuver. To execute this move, push your sibling facedown onto his or her stomach. Sit on the defender's back, facing your sibling's head. Reach down and take one of your sibling's wrists in each hand. Now put one knee between your sibling's shoulder blades and pull both arms back as hard as you can. The awkward pose and resulting squawking noises should remind everyone of that graceful predatory bird that is the symbol of our great nation.

Antagonize

Big showy maneuvers are awfully fun, but in many situations the presence of parental referees will limit the number of potential attacks. That's why another class of techniques exist for situations when the family is watching television and parents aren't paying much attention. These are the small, crippling moves that will enrage your sibling but leave no trace that you are the real culprit.

Ear Flip

Cock your middle finger by shoving it behind the base of your thumb (use your other hand if necessary). Now bring your hand close to your sibling's earlobe and sharply release your middle finger with an outward flipping motion. The rapidly moving middle finger should connect painfully with the dangling earlobe. Cock both hands beforehand to deliver this move with both barrels.

Caution: This move is painful and may lead to instant retaliation.

Variation:
Ear Yank

Alternately, use your forefinger and thumb to secure the defender's earlobe and then sharply tug it downward. Only tug upward if you're prepared for a serious fight. Either way, this move is best performed on the run so that you'll have a head start.

Foot Shove

Assume a relaxed stance directly in front of your sibling. Feint movement with your arms while placing one foot over one of your sibling's feet with all of your weight. (The goal here is not to stomp or cause foot pain, but to pin your sibling to the spot.) With your sibling's foot properly anchored, give him a shove. Unable to stand and yet not able to fall, your unbalanced sibling will likely windmill his arms and cry pathetically.

Variation:
Foot Stomp

Avoid all the complicated shoving and just stomp your foot down onto your sibling's toes. This is good to use when in a hurry, or when your sibling is unwisely barefoot while you've got on shoes.

Pinch

Grab your sibling's skin between your thumb and forefinger and squeeze tightly. For maximum pain, pinch the sensitive skin on the back of an arm or leg. This quick attack is hard for parents to detect and if done properly does not leave a mark.

Variation:
Horse Bite

Push your thumb out between your forefinger and middle finger, and make a fist. Now wiggle your thumb back and forth and wave your hand around menacingly. Without further effort on your part, anybody who gets close to your gyrating thumb will earn a nasty pinch. Use this move in a place where your sibling can't escape (like in the car, in a tree house, or in a restaurant) and enjoy terrorizing and injuring your sibling at the same time.

Trip

Few Bro-Jitsu moves are simpler or more gratifying than sticking your foot out in front of your sibling and watching him trip and sprawl on the ground. Nothing, that is, except saying afterward, "Have a nice trip? See you next fall." The most straightforward approach is to position yourself in front of your sibling, put one leg out, and forcibly shove your victim over the outstretched leg. Other approaches are more subtle.

Variations:
Flat Tire

Follow close behind a walking sibling. Place the toe of your shoe on the heel of his shoe just as his foot is going down. As he lifts his foot to take a step, your toe will tear the shoe off the back of his foot. Feel free to repeat this move seconds after your sibling has laboriously put his shoe back on.

Caution: This move is highly annoying—expect retaliation.

Heel Kick

Follow directly behind a walker. When he lifts a foot to take a step, kick the bottom of his shoe straight up. This will not send the defender sprawling to the ground, but will cause great dis-combobulation. If done properly, you can turn a normal-walking sibling into a dorky high-stepper.

Heel Trip

Use this move when a sibling is trying to run away or just walking obliviously nearby. Watch her stride carefully. The instant she has one foot raised, knee bent—kick her heel toward her

other leg. The kicked foot will catch behind the opposite knee and your sibling will no longer be bipedal.

Kneel Trip

Team up with another sibling to perform this classic maneuver. One attacker crouches on all fours behind the intended victim, and the other attacker shoves the defender. As the defender tries to balance, the unexpected presence of a human speed bump will send him sprawling.

Caution: If the intended victim notices the crouched sibling before being shoved, the crouched attacker is at risk of receiving a kick to the stomach.

Weak Knee

Sneak up behind a sibling who is standing still with her knees locked. Sharply, but gently, kick the back of her knee. The sudden loss of support will send her hands flying out for balance and will startle her in a really deeply satisfying way.

Wet Willy

To instigate a quick fight: lick your forefinger so that it is glistening with saliva. Next, stick your finger directly into your sibling's ear. If you have the time and the inclination, wiggle your finger around and shout, "Wet willy!"

Variations:
Dry Willy
Skip the licking step for a faster move that is less likely to cause a fight.

Bug in Your Ear
A frightening variant is to sneak up behind an unwary sibling, reach close to her ear, and then slide your thumb hard across the side of your curved index finger. With practice, the insectile noise and vibration will startle and terrify.

Turn the Humiliation Up to Eleven

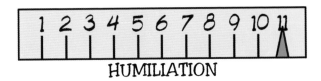

Bro-Jitsu battles will continue nonstop throughout your entire childhood—and that can last for years. Thus, it is no surprise that the bulk of offensive Bro-Jitsu moves focus less on short-term physical incapacitation and more on the long-term destruction of the will to live in others. Follow these instructions to humiliate your siblings without injuring them too severely. This way, they'll be ready for fresh humiliation bright and early the next morning.

Hairy Mon

Tackle your sibling and assume the *shoulder pin* position, trapping him on his back and facing up at you. Use both of your hands to pin his arms securely, and then lean forward and push the top of your head into his face. Twist your neck back and forth, rubbing your hairy noggin directly into his face. For the victim, this move feels sort of like eating an armpit.

Countermove:
Bite

Nothing will stop a *hairy mon* faster than taking a bite out of your sibling's haircut—but is it really worth it? Not if he uses hair gel.

Noogie

Starting from *headlock* position, place the knuckles of your free hand on the crown of your sibling's head. Now rub vigorously until you hear a *squeal*.

Variation:
Hair Muss

For a more friendly move, use an open palm instead of your knuckles. This will mess up carefully combed hair while not causing any serious pain to a sibling who might have a delicate dome, like your little sister.

Pink Belly

This move is best performed with the entire family aligned against one unlucky sibling. One attacker yanks up the defender's shirt and everyone joins together in blissful familial harmony, slapping the sibling's unprotected belly over and over again until it turns a bright shade of pink.

Variation:
Raspberry

Instead of slapping like mad, lean in and blow fart noises onto your sibling's exposed soft, fleshy belly. The tickling will be nearly unbearable and the resulting noises are both laugh- and shame-inducing.

Countermove:
Full-Body Defensive Fish Wiggle

This chaotic, wiggling move makes it difficult for giggling family members to target your vulnerable underbelly. (See page 71.)

Stop Hitting Yourself

This classic move requires that you overpower your sibling. Grab your sibling by her wrists and repeatedly shove her hands into her face. In a sympathetic tone, beg your sibling to stop hitting herself. The pain of being hit in the face will be overshadowed by her indignity at knowing she's doing it with her own hand.

Caution: If the sibling is too strong, wait until he or she is laughing really hard to make your move.

Variation:
Stop Picking Your Own Nose and Trying to Eat It

By virtue of its name this move is considered self-explanatory, along with *stop picking your butt, stop touching the cat's butt,* and *stop hitting Mom.*

Nipple Cripple

This popular move has many other names, such as the *purple nurple* or *tune in to Tokyo.* No matter what you call it, the move involves grabbing your brother's nipples and delivering a sharp twist. Depending on the situation, it may be appropriate to target both nipples at once, or to perform the attack through a T-shirt.

Caution: Under no circumstances should the nipple cripple be used against sisters.

Variation:
Fake Nipple

For a related unisex move, grasp your sister's shirt with two hands in the chest area and pinch the fabric. Twist the shirt violently and yank it back and forth. When you let go, your sibling will be unharmed, but her damaged shirt will sport two misshapen, lumpy nipples of fabric that will remain until the garment is washed. To triple the humiliation, perform this move just before school starts so she will have a pair of cringe-inducing super-nips visible all day.

Wedgie (aka Snuggy)

This move offers a perfect combination of searing pain and blushing humiliation. With an exaggerated prancing motion, sneak up silently behind the victim. In one smooth, fast movement—reach down the back of his pants, grab his underwear, and yank upward with all of your might. Laugh to yourself as your sibling runs away screaming with a tail of stretched-out underwear hanging behind.

Countermove:
Wedgie-Proof Underwear

By pre-cutting the seam of your underwear, it is possible to preserve your precious bits and pieces, if not your dignity, from a wedgie attack. Use scissors to add strategic horizontal snips along the back seam and add a vertical snip to the front of the seam. When an attacker yanks the underwear, the seam will rip completely off, leaving an opportunity for cowardly flight.

Summon the Forces of Insanity

Bro-Jitsu is as much about flair as technique. For this reason, a certain class of moves depend upon massive intimidation rather than a dazzling offense. Wait until parental referees are absent or the babysitter has her back turned and your sibling knows that nobody is coming to the rescue. A terrified enemy is easier to defeat, so choose style over substance and use the following moves to unleash the fury inside you.

Chin Drill

Reach up to your face and turn an imaginary key or start an imaginary chain saw. Thrust out your chin and begin to make a loud buzzing noise. Watch your sibling's eyes widen in horror as your "chin drill" comes up to speed. At the moment of maximum terror, tackle your sibling and dig your chin into weak points, such as the neck or kidneys.

Dogpile

A family favorite since time immemorial, this move depends on teaming up on a single sorry sibling. The

dogpile is generally
invoked by a shout. For
example, to bury a whiny
little sister under a mountain of writhing family members, just shout, "Dogpile on Anna!" Now leap onto the
defender like it's the last second of the Super Bowl.

Variations:
Steamroller

Lie down on the floor with your arms at your
sides. After a couple of practice wiggles, roll
your entire body with abandon and crush all

that lies in your path—with luck, a little sister or two.

Tackle

Why let your family have all the fun? Scream like a banshee and run toward your sister. Now leap into the air, grab ahold of her, and use your dead weight to drag her onto the floor. Tackle accomplished.

Hot Ears

Extend your arms in front of you and hold your open palms completely flat. Place one palm on each of your sibling's ears and rub vigorously. Although this extremely satisfying move has no immediate effect, it will leave a sibling with uncomfortably hot, throbbing ears for up to thirty minutes after completion.

Caution: This move is prohibited if earrings are present—ouch.

Variation: Hot Face

Perform the *hot ears* maneuver to the cheeks. Be careful not to poke anybody's eye out.

Wrist Burn

Another wonderful application of friction: grasp your sibling's forearm with both hands. Then rapidly twist your hands in opposite directions as though you are wringing water from a dishrag. After just a few sharp twists, your sibling will be shouting in pain with a red, glowing forearm.

Typewriter

Hold out your arm, extend your index finger, and stiffen it. Alternately, use the index finger and middle finger together for more strength. Now repeatedly jab your sibling in the middle of the chest, increasing intensity with each jab and saying out loud, "Dit, dit, dit." After a dozen or so jabs, shout "Ding!" and lightly smack your sibling upside the head. This maneuver reproduces the use of an archaic device called a "typewriter"—it's like a computer keyboard combined with a printer that doesn't use electricity.

Windmill

Assume a relaxed stance in the middle of the room. Extend your arms straight out from your sides, ball your hands into fists, and spin in rapidly accelerating circles. Nearby siblings will be in danger of being destroyed by your spinning cyclone of terror, especially as you begin to lose your balance.

Caution: When this move is delivered to a big brother by a little sister, the windmill will likely strike at an uncomfortable height.

Countermove:
Windmill

It is a well-known Bro-Jitsu fact that only another windmill can stop the first windmill.

Scenario:
Bro-Jitsu in the Pool

Sibling rivalry can happen anywhere, not just at home, at school, or in the car. It pays to be prepared for anything, and that includes using your Bro-Jitsu skills in an aquatic environment. In the summertime, the swimming pool is a great place to take things up a notch, as the watery environment allows the use of normally taboo moves like *spitting loogies* and *de-pantsing*, while also making room for lung-filling splash attacks. During the afternoon free swim, after your prey have been marinating in chlorinated water for hours, is the perfect time for you to go on the offense.

Breath-Holding Competition

Challenge your over-competitive sibling to a breath-holding competition—whoever holds his breath the longest wins. The instant he goes under the water, get out of the pool, dry off, and go inside. He wins.

Candy Bar

The swimming pool is a great place to gross out your siblings. A technique used in an ancient movie called

Caddyshack involves dropping an unwrapped chocolate candy bar in the pool. The floating brown object will get a reaction from everyone in the pool, especially when you casually swim over to the floater, pick it up, and take a bite out of it.

Variations:
Infected Band-Aid

Inevitably, somebody enters the pool wearing a Band-Aid. After a few minutes the disgusting little bandage will be waterlogged and full of pus. Now is the perfect time to flick it onto your sibling's back, where it will stick (hopefully unnoticed, for hours).

Misinformation

The slightly exotic terrain of the swimming pool presents an opportunity to fill your siblings' heads with outrageous lies, some of which they may continue to believe well into adulthood.

For example, did you know that if you pee in the pool, there is a chemical that will turn the water bright red? No? Well, then you probably also didn't know that alligators live under the grates at the bottom of the pool, dummy.

Cannonball

Assume a relaxed stance on a diving board or next to the deep end of the swimming pool. Locate your poolside target(s), determine your splash radius, and then aim for a close landing. Next, using all of your momentum, leap into the air and curl your body into a dense ball—knees tucked up to your chest, your arms wrapped around them, and your hands clasped together tightly. Your impact should send a spray of chilly, chlorinated pool water directly onto the screaming targets.

Variation: Shove

If the goal is to completely soak a sibling, just shove him into the swimming pool. This takes careful planning, as a determined sibling is next to impossible to shove, nudge, or carry into the pool. Wait until he is near the edge and distracted, then dart in with a quick shove to the upper body. Step back quickly—you don't want to get dragged into this impromptu pool party.

Dunk

This classic pool maneuver interferes with your siblings' crucial ability to breathe. The most straightforward approach is to leap partially out of the water, place both hands on a sibling's shoulders, and press down with all of your weight. A more aggressive approach calls for grabbing your sibling's head with both hands and dragging it under.

Caution: Release before the bubbles stop.

Variations:
Fake Left, Fake Right, Splash, Dunk!

For either dunking approach, success rates increase with a little deception up front. As the name of this move implies, it helps to extend both arms to the left, then to the right, and send up a splash (toward the eyes), before finally leaping forward for the dunk.

Shark Grab

A dunk can come from above or below. To perform a shark grab, wait until your sibling isn't paying attention and then quietly slide deep underwater. Near the pool bottom, swim directly beneath your sibling. Then quickly grab a foot with both hands and yank her under.

Caution: You aren't really a shark, so no biting.

Splash

The splash is a classic pool move that can be executed in a variety of ways for many purposes. The most popular splash technique is to use both hands to send a targeted blast of water into your sibling's face. In any depth of water, put both hands together, palms out. Several configurations work. Now shove your palms forward, skimming the surface of the water and generating a targeted splash.

Variations:
Cover Splash

A cover splash can be performed with hands or feet and is used to create confusion during a getaway. Beat the surface of the water with your limbs like an insane zoo ape. Don't stop until the pool is frothy.

Hand Squirt

Clasp your hands together so that the fingertips on each hand curl around the forefinger area of the other hand—sort of like shaking your own hand. Pull your palms slightly apart so that a hole appears on top, in between your thumbs. Fill this small, watertight cup with water and then contract your hands to shoot a stream of water from the hole. Aim the squirt toward your sibling's eyes, ears, or open mouth.

Swipe Splash

Assume a relaxed stance in waist-deep water. Extend both hands just above the water surface and slightly cup both palms. Lower one hand at a time and sharply swivel your hips to shoot a spray of water forward. Rotate back and forth to keep up a continuous, devastating spray that comes from both the left and right.

Towel Snap

Using two hands, pick up a towel by the corners and twist it lengthwise until it looks like a rope. Dip both ends into the pool until they are damp. Holding each end of the

towel in one hand, pull the twisted towel taut. Now simultaneously let go with one hand and use the other hand to yank the towel toward yourself—this will cause the rear end of the towel to "snap" forward like a whip. After delivering a snap, grab both ends and spin the towel like a jump rope to quickly wind it back into snapping position. Repeat until siblings are covered in red marks.

DEFENSIVE MOVES

In a typical demonstration of Bro-Jitsu, it may seem as though there is no danger, or even as if the participants are enjoying themselves. Nothing could be further from the truth. In reality, Bro-Jitsu is a life-or-death struggle in which a system of reflexively employed defensive maneuvers are all that keep participants from suffering a grisly dismemberment.

In this chapter, we cover an intricate series of defensive techniques that have been invented and perfected (mostly by little brothers and sisters) over the course of human history and prehistory. Mastering proper defense is an essential skill for everyone, whether it is a younger sibling biding her time for a psychological attack or a big brother who simply needs to protect his precious 'nards. These defensive moves balance out the offensive attacks so that the cycle of Bro-Jitsu can continue for years on end without serious injury.

Slow the Attack

No matter how strong your offense, it is sometimes necessary to employ defensive maneuvers that will deflect incoming attacks, force your sibling into vulnerable positions, or tire him out. When an offensive barrage of Bro-Jitsu comes raining down, it pays to know the basic moves that will slow that thunderstorm to a drizzle.

Butt Block

Enraged siblings will often charge into an attack. With little time to react, it is best to stick with your first instinct and place your most padded body part between yourself and your attacker. As the sibling nears, spin around and stick out your heinie. With luck, he will bounce harmlessly away from your padded defensive posterior, giving you valuable time to prepare a counterattack.

Chicken Wing

In many circumstances an incoming *punch* will be

announced well before it arrives. Siblings may telegraph their moves by cocking a fist and wagging it in the air, spotting Volkswagen Beetles before we do, or by announcing their intentions out loud in English. To deflect an incoming blow, turn your body to one side and stick out your elbow. Wiggle (you might say flap) one elbow up and down rapidly to present a quick shield that will hurt the attacker's fist.

Crazy Legs

The most dangerous body part in Bro-Jitsu is not the fist, the knee, or even the elbow; it's the rounded ball of bone that you walk around on all day—the heel. To execute this defensive move, fall onto your back (preferably on a couch) and kick your legs wildly in the air. Be sure to keep your heels thrust out and jabbing in random directions. Nothing says "bone bruise" like trying to fight your way through a flurry of sharp heels.

Countermoves:
Windmill

If your goal is to get past the *crazy legs* defense, then only one move will work. A strong windmill spinning attack will push your sibling's crazy legs to the side, leaving him as vulnerable as an open clam.

Butt Block

Properly timing a *windmill* counter can be difficult. Instead, a novice may try smothering the defender with a butt block in order to close the distance to his opponent.

Defensive Hop Kick

Lift one leg and hold out your foot threateningly, as though you are about to kick. Using your leg as both an offensive threat and a defensive shield, hop forward quickly. Once in range, grab your sibling with your hands and employ whatever offensive move you like.

Full-Body Defensive Fish Wiggle

This move comes naturally to younger siblings (as well as to fish) and it is useful in nearly any defensive situation. From a prone position on the ground, wiggle your entire body back and forth violently and flail your limbs without any regard to whom you might head-butt, elbow, or kick. Also, close your eyes and holler. That way, if you accidentally knock a sibling's tooth loose during the FBDFW, it isn't your fault.

Forehead Hold

This move is appropriate for use against younger, smaller siblings (or ones with abnormally short arms). As the attacker approaches, extend one arm with the elbow slightly bent and the palm out. When your sibling is within range, place your palm firmly against her forehead and press outward. This will keep some distance between your body and a wildly swinging little sister.

Settle Disagreements

The world of Bro-Jitsu is vicious, and nowhere is this primal ferocity more obvious than in Games of Chance. These moves are perfect for wrapping up battles, choosing who gets what, and for wasting time while waiting for the bus to school. These settling moves don't require any equipment or extra paraphernalia—just your poor beaten-up paws and the steely will to prevail.

Bloody Knuckles

The rules of this game are simple: each combatant makes a fist and then the fists punch each other. You flinch, you lose. Whoever lasts the longest before quitting wins. Be sure to keep your thumb outside your fist and wrapped around your fingers (so as not to break it) and angle your knuckles down so that the bony protrusions are the first to impact. This will decrease wear and tear on your finger bones and increase the amount of pain you inflict.

Mercy

For siblings who are well-matched in wrist strength, this game becomes about who can stand more wrist agony. Clasp hands with your sibling, fingers interlocked, and palms pushed together perpendicular to the ground. (Be sure to use both hands to even the odds if one sibling is left-handed and the other right-.) On the count of three, the game of mercy begins. With all your might, bend your wrists forward and your sibling's backward. Pushing will hurt in between your fingers, but the pain is much less than having your wrists bent backward at unnatural angles. The loser concedes by dramatically dropping to his or her knees and literally shouting for "mercy!"

Pencil Break

Sometimes the noble pencil may act as a substitute for preadolescent rage. The game of pencil break works like this: flip a coin to determine who goes first. The loser holds out a pencil horizontally, firmly holding both ends in his fists. The winner holds his pencil above and delivers a well-practiced downward flick designed to break the other pencil in half. Players alternate turns until someone's pencil breaks. If you're left with a whole pencil, you just won the game.

Rock, Paper, Scissors (aka Roshambo)

Some version of rock, paper, scissors has been around for as long as siblings have (although modern scissors were only invented in 1761). On the count of three, both players make a hand gesture at the same time. A fist signifies a rock, two outstretched fingers signify scissors, and a flat palm indicates paper. Rock smashes scissors. Scissors cut paper. Paper covers rock. Simplicity is key to the success of this game.

Note: This game is not random—with practice it is possible to predict a sibling's every choice, so commit some brainpower to outguessing your simpler sib.

Countermove:
Double Bluff

Announce out loud what your next move is going to be. Your sibling won't believe that you'll actually do it, so when you do and she loses, you will have pulled the wool with a double bluff.

Slap Hands

One of the more painful settling games requires quick reflexes and a stomach for severe hand pain. Flip a coin to determine who goes first. The loser places both hands out at waist level, palms down. The winner places both hands just beneath the loser's, palms up. The two lock eyes, and the winner tries to flip both hands around and over to viciously slap the top of the loser's hands. If the loser dodges by pulling both hands back, it's now her turn. But if the defender is "faked out"—the attacker was only feinting and the defender moved her hands prematurely—then the defender receives a dreaded "free hit" to the top of her hands.

Note: Depending on the rules, up to three fake-outs may be required before a free hit is earned.

Thumb Wrestling

In this one-handed game, opposing siblings curl the four fingers of one hand together tightly, leaving their thumbs hovering upward like swaying sea monsters ready to do sea-monster battle. The formal declaration of engagement is as follows: "One, two, three, four, I declare a thumb war!" The first player who is able to pin the other person's thumb down for an out-loud count of three is the winner.

Note: In some areas, the word "pinochle" (pronounced "pee-knuckle") is substituted for "thumb."

Variation:
Trap Door

In more complicated versions of thumb war, some extra fingers may get involved in the action. Commonly called a trap door, *snake*, or a *buddy*—this is a technique where the index finger may be used as surprise leverage. Remember to call this maneuver before the game starts (i.e., say, "Trap door"), otherwise its use is assumed to be forbidden.

Goad (Don't Fight)

No matter how tough your sibling may be, the ultimate authority in the room will always be the parental referee. Whether they wield their power through guilt, threats, or plain old-fashioned respect—the parents have the final say in Bro-Jitsu. But just like any referee, parental referees can be fooled, tricked, and misled to your own advantage. That's why it is often best to use a quickly delivered goad to force your enraged sibling into a full-on attack where parental referees can catch her.

Dork Face

While a *smirk* can pour salt in an existing wound, making an extremely gross dork face can cause hurt feelings all by itself. Every accomplished Bro-master has his or her own unique favorite dork face, so here are some tips for getting started on your own. First, determine if you've got any anatomical mutations. Can you turn your eyelids inside out? Bend your ears backward? Flip your lips upside down, whatever that means? If so, then do all of that. Next, use your hands to either stretch out some part of your face or to make a silly gesture. For example, make circles with your forefingers and thumbs, then hold the gesture up to your face like glasses. When parental referees look, quickly revert back to normal.

Heavy Breathing

Before you've brushed your teeth in the morning, find your sibling and deliver this antagonizing move. Put your face inches from your sister's nose, close your eyes, and exhale heavily. In some cases, it might help to pretend that you are asleep. Other times, it might make more sense to say something breathy, such as this line from an old breath mint commercial: "Heckuva hot tub, huh, Heather?"

Only Looking

Stare fiercely, but do not touch. When your sibling complains, it will only annoy your parents. Lean in closer and don't blink. When your enraged sibling attacks, it will technically be unprovoked. After all, you were "only looking."

Variation:
I'm Not Touching You!

This immensely satisfying technique is simple and elegant. Put your finger directly in front of your sibling's face, but don't touch. Pretend there is a force field hovering three inches away from your sibling and poke it, rub it, and nudge it—but never touch skin. This move is guaranteed to

enrage a sibling of any age or gender within thirty seconds, all without technically touching anybody and violating the precious "rules" laid out by parental referees.

On My Side

Something mysterious and special happens whenever two siblings are within sight of each other—an invisible line appears midway between them. These lines have been known to appear between siblings sitting next to each other on the living room couch, the backseat of the car, or across from each other at the dinner table. Crossing this line is an obvious offense to brothers and sisters, but parents are completely blind to it. Take advantage and place your foot or hand slightly—just slightly—over the imaginary line. When your sibling complains and then attacks, you'll notice that, to your benefit, parents just don't understand.

Parrot

A simple and effective move for younger siblings is to repeat whatever your older sibling says, preferably in an annoying tone. To add icing to the cake, copy facial expressions and gestures.

Caution: Always switch the pronoun when your sibling inevitably delivers an insult to himself in an attempt to make your move backfire. For example, after your sibling says "I'm a little idiot," be sure to translate this to "You're a little idiot."

Smirk

The sting of any slight insult can be magnified by a well-placed smirk. Unlike a smile—which exhibits genuine happiness—the smirk is a sharp, mean-spirited expression that screams "Ha ha, you lose!" This brat-smile can easily push your sibling over the line when she is teetering on the brink of attack. Just make sure parental referees are nearby to catch the counterattack.

Variation:
Boo Hoo

In total silence, make an exaggerated sad face and cock your head slightly to the side. Now raise both fists to your eyes and rub them on your cheeks. Shudder as if you are crying and in a high falsetto, croon the words "boo hoo." In the worst-case scenario, your sibling will actually break down in tears, and in the best case he will rush into an ill-advised attack.

Call in the Parental Cavalry

Goading is a great way to encourage a parental referee to do your dirty work. However, bear in mind that most parents work for free and hardly ever take time off from refereeing continuous Bro-Jitsu matches. It is no surprise, then, that parental referees will eventually start to ignore noncritical Bro-Jitsu situations. For this reason, an entire class of Bro-Jitsu moves have emerged to force indifferent parents to fulfill their refereeing duties.

Don't Break My Glasses!

Loudly mentioning valuable items that may be broken during a fight—items that your parents will have to pay to replace—is likely to get the attention of apathetic parental referees who have been pushed beyond the ability to care about your physical or mental health.

Note: This move only works if you wear glasses (or expensive, stylish sunglasses).

Preemptive Cry of Pain

In the seconds (or minutes) before an attack, cry out in heart-wrenching agony. This will likely get your parents' attention even before the blow lands. Your sibling will stand stupefied as parental wrath comes crashing down on his innocent head. As for technique, the more your cry makes it sound like you broke your arm, the better.

Caution: Do not overuse this technique, lest you suffer the fate of the boy who cried "Wolf!"

Variation:
Fake Crying

When the fight looks bleak and unwinnable, do what comes natural—burst uncontrollably into tears. If your sibling turns repentant, immediately *sucker punch* him in the stomach and *scamper* away. Otherwise, wait for the parental cavalry to arrive.

Re-peat, Re-peat, Re-peat

Sometimes quantity outweighs quality. Get your parents' attention by repeating a call for attention over and over. For example, "Mommy, Mom, Mother, Mommo." Be sure to vary the speed and volume, otherwise a parental referee might become used to your monotonous, never-ending plea for attention.

Note: In extremely desperate situations, use your parent's first name (if you know it).

Squeal

An annoying, high-pitched keen might attract the attention of exhausted parents who would normally ignore your desperate pleas for help. If your shout breaks a glass vase, you're doing it right.

Countermove:
Stifle

Quiet a squealing little sister with a hand over her mouth.

Counter-countermove:
Hand Lick

Lick the stifler's hand.

Counter-counter-countermove:
Smear

Wipe your freshly licked hand all over the defender's face.

Countermove

Counter-countermove

Counter-counter-countermove

Live to Fight Another Day

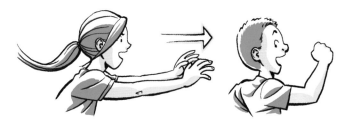

Not every fight can be won—sometimes a Bro-battle has gone too far, parental referees have left you alone for too long, or all the fun and energy has been sapped from your weary young bones. To reduce the time spent as a human punching bag, the following desperate escape sequences may have to be enacted. These moves aren't pretty, but they get the job done.

Beg

If you haven't got any integrity left, just cave in and beg for mercy. Keep in mind that your sibling will instantly recognize your pathetic defeat and will push you as far as possible, asking you to extol his or her own virtues while describing what a sad coward you are. Just keep your fingers crossed behind your back and remember that every minute spent begging is a minute spent without fists pounding into your shoulder.

Give It

The first law of Bro-physics is stated as follows: anything

you've got, your sibling wants to take away from you. As such, the phrase "Give it" is used a lot between siblings. If you are on the receiving end and the fight isn't worth it, go ahead and comply. But before you "give it"—whatever it is—lick it first.

Possum

Run for it and find some bedcovers. Climb under them, wrap yourself up like a child-size burrito, and play dead. Your attacker will likely kick and punch your padded form for a little while. There is a good chance, however, that your sibling will quickly grow bored with attacking a silent, limp body bag.

Caution: Be sure to make an air vent so that you can breathe.

Variation: Turtle

If you don't have time to run, fall to the ground on your stomach. Curl into a fetal position and pull your shirt over your head. Lie there pretending to be dead.

Scamper

Bro-scientists define scamper as the fastest run possible while wearing socks on hardwood floors. As you scamper away, be sure to close doors behind you, throw pillows in your pursuer's path, and be on the lookout for a couch or chair to leap onto for a transition to the highly defensive prone *crazy legs kick*. Ultimately, you might just tire out your sibling so that she is too weak to beat you once she catches you.

Variation:
Run for Mom

A mother's skirt can be as powerful as a brick wall. Dads are not a safe bet, however, as they are more likely to join in the fun of picking on weaker siblings.

Tell on Your Siblings

The most powerful way for a smaller, weaker sibling to leverage the authority of parental referees is simple— tell. The art of telling is more complicated than it seems, however. Without the proper technique, the value of telling declines quickly as parental referees lose their patience. In addition, the style of telling can influence the severity of the punishment. Learn to squeal on your siblings correctly and you will become a Bro-master without ever lifting a finger.

Faux Confession

Use this move only if you are the sibling that your parents trust most. As a trusted source, you may occasionally come forward and "confess" a humiliating, made-up fact about your less trustworthy sibling. For example, tell your mother that your brother has a strange rash on his butt and is too embarrassed to mention it to anyone. Now go play Barbie dolls while your frustrated sibling tries to explain himself in vain.

Ooh, I'm Telling!

Telling on someone is a great way to get her in trouble while becoming a hero at the same time. Just remember that every tell comes at a cost—parental referees get tired of upholding the law and you risk being branded a "tattletale" among your friends. Instead, just threaten to tell. This way you get what you want from your sibling without the cost associated with approaching a parental referee. Of course, as a little extortionist, you also aren't at risk of becoming a hero anytime soon.

Straight Tell

The straight tell consists of running to a parent at top speed and reporting the extremely illegal and immoral behavior of your siblings. This move is also liable to get old with parental referees disturbingly fast. Follow these tips to increase the power and longevity of your telling:

 Show, don't tell. A tell will have more impact if it isn't accompanied by obvious malice on your part. For example, instead of running off to show your parents a new bruise, just make sure they see it and ask you about it. Now you can tearfully rat out your sibling from beneath a pure golden halo. Carry on, you bruised little saint.

Alternate between parents. Each parent has a different-size reservoir of patience for putting up with you and your sister. If Mom has had enough, go tell Dad. Once Dad has been pushed to the limit, switch back to Mom.

Tailor your tell. Sometimes the dramatic intensity of your story matters more than what really happened. Be sure to tie in important facts or recent newsworthy events. For example, instead of saying "John broke the lamp," say that "John destroyed the lamp like terrorists destroyed our nation's sense of security. And it was the lamp that always reminded me of a mother's love for her children."

Tell at the right time. Choose the perfect time to deliver a tell for maximum impact. For example, never tell on your brother the second your dad walks in the door from work. Offer Dad a frosty cold beverage first, and then take him on a trip down to tattle-town.

Scenario:
Bro-Jitsu in the Car

For siblings who are used to being on the defense, the car can be the perfect place to strike back. Having parents close by and physical impediments like seat belts affords special opportunities and levels the playing field. With clever seat choice, timing, and selective manipulation of parental attention, a trained Bro-Jitsuer may significantly antagonize siblings while at the same time averting guilt and causing friction between parents and hapless enemy sibs.

Call Shotgun!

Don't forget to shout this word the second all siblings have exited the house in order to secure the coveted front seat. It's a whole new world up there in the front— with a better view, a more comfortable seat, and a more remote chance of being puked on by your carsick little sister. If you are slow on the draw and must sit in the backseat, avoid the center seat at all costs. It allows no access to windows and requires sitting with your feet on the hump.

Defensive Seating

Bro-Jitsu in the car (sometimes called "Car-até" followed by a groan) begins before you leave the house. The passenger seat is often unjustly denied to younger siblings, so rear seats may be the only option. The key to maintaining your health is to always sit directly behind the driver's seat. Inevitably, the parental referee driving the car will become agitated and reach back to blindly swipe at children in the rear seat (called a hand flail). The architecture of the human elbow prevents the flail attack from reaching the kid crouched behind the driver's seat.

Offensive Seating

Sitting in the front seat allows for several methods of torturing siblings trapped in the back. The easiest is to loudly praise how wonderful it feels to sit in the front seat. Afterward, be sure to set the radio dial to something that appears innocent to your parents but will make your siblings' ears bleed. And with access to the air conditioner and heater, here is your chance to either cook or freeze your siblings—or both in alternating waves. Most of all, enjoy the front seat—you deserve it!

Road Goad

Any goad delivered while in the car becomes a road goad. Wait until there are no eyes watching in the rear-view mirror and then deliver any of the standard goads: *on my side*, *smirk*, *only looking*, or *I'm not touching you*. When the sibling attacks, your parent will be near enough to smack him dizzy with a hand flail.

Seat-Belt Hang

In certain notorious situations, a spoiled sibling may be given the front seat while other more deserving children are banished to the dreaded backseat. Take heart—several counter-shotgun methods exist to inflict misery on front seat-hogging siblings. Staying mindful of hand flails, sit directly behind your sibling. After he snaps on his seat belt, grab the strap up high and pull it backward. Now hang on it with all of your weight. The strap will tighten across your brother's chest and crush the air from his smug lungs.

Variations:
Neck Tickle

A sibling safely buckled up and sitting in the front seat is uniquely susceptible to a tickle on the neck. Alternately, improvise with a *wet willy*, *ear flip*, or *hair pull*, depending on the appropriateness of the situation and, of course, your mood.

Seat-Belt Sling

Seat-belt buckles are a perfect (and obvious) weapon. Grab the belt, give it some slack, and start swinging your newfound mace.

Caution: Don't sling the belt unless you are ready to chip your brother's tooth and go live with Grandma for a few weeks.

Silent But Deadly

To antagonize everyone in the car—just cut the cheese. Ideally, your attack should be silent but deadly, so that you can blame it on your siblings (or your dad). If someone complains, wisely mention that either "The smeller's the feller" or "He who smelt it, dealt it."

Slugbug!

The passive-aggressive game of slugbug allows any sibling who spots a Volkswagen Beetle to call out the color and *punch* another sibling in the shoulder. For example, if a yellow Beetle passes by, point at it and shout "Slugbug yellow!" and then let loose with a completely legal blow to the shoulder. Technically, your sibling cannot retaliate until spotting another Volkswagen Beetle.

Taunts

In humid climes, a layer of condensation may form on the inside of car windows. Take advantage of this and use your finger to spell out insults or create humorous drawings to taunt your siblings. Alternately, write insults backward on the outside of a dusty car window; the taunt will hang there for miles and miles in your helpless sibling's face.

PSYCHOLOGICAL MOVES

Before rushing into a wedgie-inducing situation, a sibling combatant may well consider using brainpower instead of firepower. In this chapter, we delve into an advanced area of Bro-Jitsu that is reserved for the most psychologically damaging maneuvers. These moves do not rely on overpowering strength and offer no immediate defense; instead, they focus on mental and emotional aspects of combat, such as maintaining clear conduits to parental referees, keeping a good eye out for blackmail, and projecting a fearsome image to your enemies. (Nobody wants to tangle with the crazy kid.) By refusing to be drawn into physical combat, a wise sibling may maturely and efficiently manipulate opponents into incriminating encounters with parents or stop fights before they even begin.

Through a constant bombardment of crippling mental attacks, you will learn exactly how far you can push your siblings before being attacked. When rebuffing similar mental attacks, you will also learn how to monitor and control your own feelings of annoyance and anger. Pay careful attention: these mental powers will come in handy later in life, helping you keep your cool as you trade insults with a guy at a concert or when you deal with snotty customer service representatives.

Show 'Em Who's Boss

At some point, bigger siblings need to combine physical force with devastating psychological trauma to show their siblings one thing: who's the boss. Used correctly, these moves aren't particularly painful, but they can bruise the ego and smack down the self-esteem of the most precocious sibling.

De-Pantsing

After making sure no belts or suspenders will block your way, grab your sibling's pants firmly around the waist and yank them down. This attack works best against sweatpants, swimsuits, and pajamas.

Caution: Any amateur can perform a de-pantsing, but it takes an expert to recognize when to deliver this emotionally

crushing move. For maximum impact, do it in front of the victim's potential sweethearts, the mailman, or even Grandma.

Distraction Slap

Take a relaxed standing position directly in front of the defender. Look into your sibling's eyes, raise your right hand in the air, and wiggle it threateningly. The instant your sibling looks at your flapping fingers, deliver a light slap across his face with your other hand. Repeat, switching hands as necessary.

Note: If your sibling refuses to look at the distracting hand, slap him with it.

Lick the Floor

Push the defender's face against the floor with your palm or the bottom of your foot. Don't let her up until she licks the floor. It's recommended to do this at your grandma's house, where the ancient shag rug has absorbed the mysterious flavors of bygone years. This is a barbaric move, and yet when you see your sibling's little tongue dart out and brush against the floor—it's suddenly all worth it.

Say "Uncle"

Sure, we all enjoy hurting our siblings by sitting on them, tickling them, and twisting their little arms behind their backs. But where do we go from there? When maximum pain has been inflicted, it is time to enter humiliation territory. So whatever it is you're doing, don't stop doing it until your sibling cries out "Uncle!" in abject hopelessness.

Countermove:
Cross Your Fingers

Everyone knows that anything you say with your fingers crossed doesn't really count. So cross 'em tight and say "Uncle." But when you're free, show your crossed fingers to the attacker, laugh triumphantly, and then run like your life depends on it (because it might).

PROJECT A STRONG IMAGE

In a martial art as highly stylized as Bro-Jitsu, it's impossible to overstate the importance of posturing. Every Bro-Jitsu encounter begins when the combatants see each other and size each other up. The most accomplished Bro-Jitsuers never even have to fight because they have convinced their siblings that they are absolutely insane.

Crazy Eyes

Sadly, this move can't be learned: some of us have crazy eyes and some of us don't. For those siblings out there who can make crazy eyes, appreciate your gift. Flashing a psychotic, wild-eyed glare projects the proper image of a deranged lunatic.

Caution: If you haven't got crazy eyes, don't try to fake it—you'll just look like a freakin' dorkwad.

Fake Karate Stance

Adopt a fake karate stance—the crane kick is always a good one (balanced on one leg, arms up, other leg bent

and ready to strike). Alternately, raise your hands up slowly and breathe in through the nose loudly, then lower your hands and breathe out through your mouth. This intimidating display may make opponents think twice about fighting someone who could very well be a master of fake karate.

Growl

A low growl will let your siblings know that it's time to back off, or they will be attacked by the savage beast that lurks within you (and is presently growling).

Caution: When a little sister employs the growl, she may shatter previous cuteness records.

Variations:
Heavy Breathing

Clench your teeth together. Scowl. Now breathe loudly through your teeth and don't be shy about letting the spit fly. As a passionate, heavy-breathing berserker, you appear invulnerable and more than a little bit off your rocker.

Hiss

Quick and efficient, bare your fangs and hiss like a feral cat whenever sibs come too close.

Loom

Taller siblings can employ passive psychological torture simply by looming threateningly over smaller sibs. After months or years of torture and unexpected assaults, your stubby sibling won't be able to relax as long as you stand to her side or just behind, looming silently and radiating a poisonous ill will.

Variation: Screen

Pretend you're a pro basketball player and pull your arms in close to block a sibling's path. When he tries to walk around, scoot over to block his way. Make him *beg* to get past.

Silent Threat

Slide your index finger slowly across your throat like a knife and then point ominously at your sibling. Alternately, crack your knuckles and stare menacingly. Your piercing gaze and creepy gestures will either intimidate the defender into submission, or at least paralyze her with giggles.

Super-Strength

When someone goes too far, pushes too hard, or an insult hits too close to home—a divine flood of super-strength may be suddenly granted to the wronged individual. Under these circumstances, a tiny little sister may gain the power to pick up the family car and throw it down the block. If you've gone too far and a sib acquires super-strength, there can be only one countermove: run. Run for your sweet, sweet life.

Variation:
The Hulk Hogan

Sometimes the transition to *super-strength* is not instantaneous. In this case, the wronged party may initiate a move made famous by the wrestler Hulk Hogan. From the ground, slowly look up at your attacker and make *crazy eyes*. As you stand up, shake your head back and forth and wag your finger—NO! From this point on, each blow you absorb will only make you stronger.

Gross Out

Pushing the limits of common decency is your right and obligation over the course of a lifelong Bro-Jitsu war. The following moves depend on offending the moral and olfactory senses of your siblings—they rarely inflict physical damage. Remember that no matter how far your siblings are willing to go, as a Bro-master you must always be waiting on the other side with a booger clinging to your out-stretched finger.

Booger Finger

Pick your nose and then hold out the tainted finger—your pudgy digit is now a powerful Bro-Jitsu weapon. Paradoxically, the true power of the booger finger is psychological: never allow the boogery surface to actually touch your sibling. Instead, wave it around wildly to force defenders to run away, cringe, and scream with disgust.

Variations:
Fake Booger Wipe

Extend your index finger and jam it deep into your nose. Wiggle it around and stare threateningly at your brother. While he focuses in horror on your boogery index finger, quickly lick the tip of your middle finger. Reach out with your booger finger and go on the attack. When your brother cringes away, wipe your wet middle finger on his forehead.

Poop Wand

A related attack requires nothing more than a stick and a pile of dog poo. Stab the stick into the poo, then use your mighty magical poop wand to defeat your foolish enemies.

Caution: Never bring the poop wand indoors—it's a lawn weapon only.

Bug on You!

During the summer, it is easy to find the dried-up brown shells of locusts (technically cicadas) across many parts of the world. These shells are empty and have the smell and texture of dried leaves, but they stick to clothing and hair like atomic Velcro. Find one, stick it on your sibling where she can see it, and then unleash an unholy scream of terror. Watch gleefully as your sibling has a conniption fit trying to dislodge the harmless hexapod husk.

Note: No matter where you live, be sure to use the environment to your advantage: toss seaweed at the beach, leaves in the forest, or soggy toilet paper at a rest-stop bathroom.

Burp Blow

Belch loudly into your mouth, puffing your cheeks. Make fleeting eye contact with your sibling and, before he can react, blow the burp directly his face. If your sibling realizes the move is in progress, he may try to hold his breath. If this happens, wait until he must inhale before blowing the fetid air from your mouth.

Countermove:
Reverse Burp Blow

By performing the same move with a one-second delay, you can send a counter-burp into your sibling's nostrils just as he inhales.

Variation:
Stealth Burp Blow

Instead of making your intentions clear, gather a quiet burp in your mouth and sidle up next to your sibling. Covertly blow the burp from the corner of your mouth toward your sibling's nostrils. Now play it off like nothing happened, while your sister doubles over in sudden nausea.

Cat Butt

Find a docile house cat and gently pick it up with one hand under the chest and another under the belly. Now reverse it and set the cat on your sibling's face. There will be a split second while your sib visually identifies the cat rectum hovering inches from his or her face. Use this special moment to reflect on how glad you are to have a brother or sister.

Variation:
Dog Butt

This move is also performable with a small dog, although the dog is less likely to enjoy the maneuver than a cat.

Dutch Oven

This despicable move should be used rarely, if at all. While in bed, shove your sibling's head under the covers and hold it there. Now fart. As she struggles to escape, keep in mind that the chances of this move causing irreparable brain damage are slim, but the psychological harm is all too real.

Caution: Perform this move after eating a bean burrito and your sibling may never forgive you.

Variation:
Fart Pin

Also known as the *gas hold*. Starting from a *shoulder pin* position, inch forward until your knees are on either side of your captive sibling's head. Now lift your body slightly and drop a wicked air biscuit.

Caution: At this point, you should pray that your sibling is not a biter.

Hanging Spit Fake

Sit on your sibling's chest in the *shoulder pin* position and then lean over and let a long rope of drool dangle over the defender's face—now suck it back up before it falls! To achieve the proper soupy spit consistency, you can drink pickle juice before executing this move.

Caution: Performed incorrectly, an errant spit fake can enrage even the smallest little sister, imbuing her with a great and terrible super-strength.

Variations:
Fake Loogie

Snort loudly and crinkle your face up in a disgusting pretend display of cooking up a gooey green loogie. Now open your mouth into a small "O," blow out a stream of air, and block the opening for a split second by pushing your tongue forward, then back. The sudden start and stop of air will feel to your sibling exactly as if someone has hawked a big loogie—especially if you've done a good job convincing her that you've got one in your mouth. To complete the sticky illusion, react with horror and disgust at the imaginary loogie you've just planted between your kid sister's eyes.

Gleek

Spitting is gross and crude, but gleeking is an elegant yet deniable way of projecting saliva onto your siblings' faces or food. Unlike spitting, gleeking is the art of shooting saliva directly out of the two saliva glands located just underneath your tongue. Learning to gleek is the hardest

part. Find a very sour food, like a lemon or a sour gummy worm, and bite into it. You'll feel the back of your tongue pucker up. Open your mouth and work your jaw up and down slightly. Soon you'll notice twin columns of saliva streaking from your gaping maw. After more training, your overactive saliva glands will be launching spitty squirts worthy of a SeaWorld dolphin.

Note: Gleeking and spitting are not the same thing—learn the difference!

Loogie Launch

Snort threateningly and gather a large, soupy loogie in your mouth—for real this time. The more gurgling noises you make, the better. Threaten to spit, but never launch the loogie— you don't want a full-out loogie fight (unless you're in a swimming pool, and then only maybe). To really gross out the defender, open up your mandible and show off your mouth snot while you try to talk.

Snot Rocket (aka Booger Blaster, Farmer Blow)

Place your index finger over one nostril and briskly blow air through your nose. A rope of snot should shoot out of your other nostril like a magnificent green rocket. Just try not to get it on your own shoes.

Pee Hands

Wash your hands after you use the toilet, but do not dry them completely. Upon leaving the bathroom, approach your sibling with your dripping fingers held out. Rub your damp hands on the hapless defender's face and/or the back of her neck. Now mention how much you hate it when you pee all over your hands.

Pull My Finger

Extend your index finger and say with a straight face, "Pull my finger." If by some cruel trick of fate your sister actually pulls your finger, immediately deliver a fart with the intensity of a subtropical storm. She should recoil in terror, unsure of whether you just filled your pants. If you aren't sure either, then congratulations— you pulled this move off perfectly.

Countermove: Back Away Slowly

When someone announces "Pull my finger," it should be obvious that you are standing next to a trouser bomb that's on a hair trigger and set to explode. Raise your arms, palms out, and back away slowly. If the bomb isn't triggered, you just might get out of this alive.

See Food?

This is a classic low-impact gross-out maneuver that can be delivered at any mealtime. Wait for parental referees to look away while you chew with your mouth properly closed. Once you have the opportunity, yank open your mouth and show your sibling the disgusting mash of half-chewed dinner rolling around your tongue. Now close it quickly—before your parents catch you!

Spitball

Take a common drinking straw and tear off the paper wrapper. Now bite off a small piece of the wrapper and chew it into a small, spit-soaked ball. Put one end of the straw into your mouth and use your tongue to push the spitty ball of paper into the straw. Now aim and blow as hard as you can.

Caution: Spitballs that hit their target will remain there as evidence, which can get you grounded.

Variations:
Iceball

Instead of chewing up pieces of paper into spitballs, just chomp on a piece of ice until it is in pieces small enough to fit into the end of the straw. The pieces of ice are harder than paper (they sting), less disgusting (no spit), and they are less likely to get you into trouble later (they melt and evaporate, leaving no evidence).

Straw Rocket

Rip off half the paper from a new straw, leaving the paper covering one end. Put the other end of the straw to your lips, aim carefully (enjoy watching siblings flinch), and then blow. The piece of paper will shoot from the straw and bounce harmlessly off the defender's face, causing mild irritation and annoyance.

Drive Them Crazy

A true student of Bro-Jitsu is in it for the long haul—this isn't a war that you can walk away from. While it is impossible to win every single battle, a determined Bro-Jitsuer can keep up a low-grade, annoying barrage of psychological tricks. Use a combination of these morale-destroying moves between major Bro-battles to loosen your siblings' hold on their own sanity while adding to your enjoyment of life.

Guess What, You're Adopted

As an older sibling, sit your kid brother or sister down for a serious talk. Break the incredible news: they were adopted from a circus family that was passing through town. Follow up this whopper with a variety of smaller backup lies: your sib's real parents were circus freaks or she was born with a tail.

Caution: This can be an especially harmful mental attack, as a kid sibling may continue to believe the news deep down for years. It is suggested that this move only be used in a family in which your kid sibling will ultimately be relieved to have been adopted.

Fake-Out

We've all got an Achilles' heel, so use your superior intellect to convince siblings that your weak spots are at the knee, elbow, and knuckles. For example, complain loudly about your sore and tender left kneecap. Instead of attacking your delicate tummy, a slow-witted sibling will proceed to rain useless blows on your most well-protected parts.

Note: This conniving trick is believed to have been invented in the 1980s by professional wrestlers who occasionally switched knee braces to the wrong knee.

Fake Poo

Nothing is more psychologically devastating than being accused of self-defecation. And nothing is more likely to bring down a tidal wave of shame on a sibling than rubbing a chocolate bar on a pair of his or her underwear and showing the gruesome "skid marks" to his friends. For an even more revolting attack, cook a chocolate bar in the microwave and pour the half-melted goo into your sibling's underwear drawer.

Variations:
Brownie Mix

For the more difficult-to-convince sibling (or the sibling who has become alert to the slightest whiff of dog poo), try scooping coffee grounds out of your mom's coffeemaker with a wet spoon. Now casually announce that you've just put some brownies in the oven and ask who wants to lick the spoon. With luck, your siblings will climb all over each other to be the first to lick the stink spoon.

Chocolate Milk

Guess what it looks like when you mix up hose water and dog poo in a bucket? Not chocolate milk so much, but a persuasive Bro-master can pull off almost anything. For an unhealthy challenge, mix up this frothy concoction in the yard, pour it into a cup, and then see if your skills of persuasion are up to the ultimate challenge of convincing your sib to drink butt gravy fresh from the yard.

Fright

Few things are more satisfying than scaring a scream or yelp from your sibling. Hide someplace: around a corner, behind a door, or under a table. When your sibling ignorantly traipses into range, leap out and howl like a rabid alley cat.

Variation:
Fright Night

Hide under your sibling's bed at the end of the evening, before he goes to sleep. You may have to keep still for half an hour or more. After your sibling turns out the lights, lies down, and starts to go to sleep . . . scratch the wall quietly. When and if your sib investigates, moan like a zombie and then grab him. Otherwise, giggle as you hear him make a panicked run for it.

I Cut Myself!

Put on an old T-shirt and pour ketchup all over your hands, arms, and chest. Now run screaming into the living room while your sibling is innocently watching cartoons. Shout things like, "Oh holy Mother Teresa, I think I cut my fingers off!" or "Dear God! Help me find my sweet

severed fingers!" Be sure to wave your bloody arms around violently and grab your kid sibling's shirt as you writhe in agony, covering her in your fake vein juice.

Nicknames

Vaguely insulting nicknames are a staple of Bro-banter (the ritualistic verbal precursor to full-on combat). Use these names to casually ramp up the anger level of your sibling.

Note: When you grow up, any of these nicknames may be used as alternative names for annoying waiters (or if you grow up to become a waiter, for annoying customers).

Ace
Amigo

Babe
Baby
Bad Boy
Big Boy
Big City
Big Country
Big Fella
Big Guy
Big Shooter
Big Shot
Big Spender
Big Time
Boss

Brah
Bro
Bud
Buddy

Captain
Casanova
Champ
Chief
Chucklehead
Chuckles
Classy
Coach
Cool Breeze
Cowboy

Daddy-o
Downtown

Fancy
Fancy Pants
Fella
Flex
Freckles

Guy

Half-Pint
Hollywood
Holmes
Homeboy
Homey
Hoss

Hot Rod
Hotshot

Jeeves

Killer
Knucklehead
Knuckles

Little Buddy

Man
Maynard
Muffin
My Main Man

Old Boy
Old Girl

Pal
Peewee
Pip-Squeak
Playboy

Player
Pop
Pumpkin

Ranger
Romeo

Sassy
Scout
Shooter
Shortie
Short Stack
Short Stuff
Sis
Sister
Skipper
Skippy
Slappy
Slick
Slim
Slugger
Smooth

Spanky
Spark Plug
Sparky
Sport
Squirt
Stretch
Sugar
Sunshine
Sweetie Pie

Tex
Tiger
Touchdown
Tough Guy
Tough Stuff
Tricks
Trixie
Twerp

Vegas

Youngblood

Taunt

Bro-scientists define taunting as the art of hurting some-one's feelings in five syllables or less. Simple descriptions related to sight and smell are completely appropriate. For example, "You smell funny" and "You know what? You're ugly" are both great taunts. Mix it up by combining some-thing gross with a body part, as in "poop face," "butt head," or "diarrhea lips." Mumble the taunt fast and quiet to keep it under the radar of parental referees. A simple rule of thumb: if a sign-language monkey would use it as an insult, then it's an okay taunt.

Variation:
Name Rhyme

Say the intended victim's name and then rhyme it with something gross or silly. It doesn't have to make sense or even rhyme very well. For example, the phrase "Daniel, Daniel is a cocker spaniel" makes little logical sense, yet still con-veys a clear sense of malice toward this Daniel character, whoever he is.

What, Are Ya Gonna Cry?

Once you've pushed too far and your poor sibling is trembling with emotion and on the verge of bursting into tears, that's the proper time to kick him while he's down with this sadistic move. As your sibling struggles to rein in his emotions, get right in his face and ask the ques-tion over and over: "What, are ya gonna cry?" If said enough times with enough emphasis on "cry," you'll be rewarded with the sweet salty tears of your tortured sibling. Was it worth it?

What's on Your Shirt?

Ask this question while you poke a finger into your sibling's chest. When she looks down at her shirt, flip your finger up and hit her in the nose. This move probably won't work more than once or twice, so be ready for a slap to the back of the head if you overuse it.

Variation:
Distraction Tap

Come up behind your sibling on one side and tap

her on the other shoulder. For example, if you are on the left, tap the right shoulder, and vice versa. While she cranes her neck around looking for you, prepare your next attack or just have a chuckle.

The Art of Bro-Jitsu
Mind Control

Against all odds, sometimes you need your sibling to do something for you: get a Popsicle from the freezer, lend a quarter, or go tell Mom that you've broken your arm and that you need an "ambliance." Since being nice to your sibling is no longer an option after years of abuse, you will need to learn a series of complicated and underhanded schemes in order to manipulate enemy siblings into doing whatever it is you want them to do.

Dare

Long ago, certain actions were considered so unbelievably stupid and dangerous that no sibling would ever even stop to think about actually performing them. These were things like jumping off the roof of your house, going underwater with a bucket on the head, or climbing into an empty cardboard box and then falling down a staircase. But then an ancient Bro-master invented the dare. By saying the magic words "I dare you," any old self-destructive behavior instantly becomes cause for upholding your honor. Once dared, a kid only has two choices: do it or chicken out.

Variations:
Double Dog Dare

Using more elaborate descriptions of the same *dare* can add a sense of escalation and growing importance, giving the *dare* more compelling strength. If the original *dare* isn't working, just use your imagination and keep adding to it so that it becomes a *double-*, *triple-*, or *infinity-duple dog dare.*

King

For the proactive sibling, just do whatever the *dare* is up front and then hold it over your sibling's head. After you declare yourself "king," your sibling will have to do whatever you did and usually a little something else. To pour salt in the wound, declare yourself the monarch of something offensive, like "King of your ugly face!"

Caution: Repeated use of this move leads to an escalation that always results in someone breaking a collarbone.

Reverse Psychology

Younger (or incredibly naive) siblings will fall for this classic approach in which you say what you don't mean. Since sibs tend to robotically do the opposite of whatever you want, why not take advantage of this? Under the premise that your sibling will do the opposite of what you say, say the opposite of what you want. For example, tell your kid brother that you hate the smell of dollar bills or that *The Little Mermaid* is the best movie ever.

Shame

Failure to comply with dangerous, nonsensical demands will be met with this demeaning move. Bend your elbows and put your hands on your hips. Now screech "Bok, bok, bok" and walk around with your head jerking back and forth until your little brother finally jumps off the high dive.

Note: Completely ignoring the shame attack is difficult but possible. Be prepared to use the strong ignore *until all your siblings have reached a mature adulthood (and maybe longer).*

Solemn Swear

Short of using physical force, it's tough to get your siblings to actually do what they say they will. Like a voodoo curse, the solemn swear capitalizes on superstitious feelings by convincing siblings that a terrible fate awaits them if they break their promise. Since this is a psychological maneuver, the more solemn and important-sounding the swear, the better it will work. So look her in the eyes and lock pinky fingers for a pinky swear, spit in your hand, and then shake, or make your sib cross her heart, hope to die, stick a needle in her eye.

Caution: That last swear is a metaphor, not to be taken literally. I mean, who wants a needle in his eye? Ouch!

Scenario: Bro-Jitsu with Little Siblings

Bro-Jitsu is a martial art practiced on some level by siblings of all ages, but most physical moves are inappropriate for use on much younger siblings. Unfortunately, kid siblings with their Kool-Aid–stained mouths and sticky hands are just as annoying as older siblings, but harder to torture. Proper Bro-Jitsu technique around kid brothers and sisters therefore requires a focus on psychological methods that take advantage of their undeveloped brains while not damaging their weak, vulnerable little bodies.

Note: All moves in this section are certified "kid-sister friendly."

Airplane

Lie on your back with your legs up. Have your little brother lean forward and rest his stomach on your feet. Take his hands in yours and lift him off the ground with your legs. This is the airplane, and although your sibling doesn't know it, life will never be this fun again. You can reduce the wholesomeness by adding turbulence and missile avoidance to this little airplane ride.

Call Santa Claus

When your kid sister is being a brat, pick up the telephone and pretend to dial up Santa Claus or any other fictional authority figure, such as the King of Cartoons, the Tooth Fairy, or SpongeBob SquarePants (or his friend Patrick, if SpongeBob is out). As your pitifully naive sibling struggles to get the phone away, turn informer on her to her greatest hero.

Note: The phone doesn't have to be plugged in. Alternately, just speak into a television remote.

Doll Mutilation

Never forget that small children are struggling to operate with underformed brains. As such, it should come as no surprise that they often attribute unusual amounts of emotion to pieces of fabric stuffed with polyurethane fibers, called dolls. (Stuffed animals also fall into the same general category.)

These puffy pals are handy vessels for punishment when your sibling is too small or delicate for such treatment. Throw the doll into a ceiling fan, hang it from the window blinds cord, or toss it down the stairs.

Variation:
Blanket Mutilation

Children are not always overinvested in dolls—sometimes filthy blankets are the objects of their affection. Take advantage of this weakness and use a "blanky" as a simulated hankie, toilet paper, or cleaning rag. If this sounds harsh, just relax—you'll be doing your little sibling a favor by teaching him an important lesson about, well, being tortured, or something.

Ear Lift

Stand behind your younger sibling and tuck your arms under her armpits. Now reach up and put your hands over her little ears. Lift the wiggling kid from the ground by the armpits, but pull dramatically on the ears to complete the mind-bending illusion that is . . . the ear lift.

Girl- or Boy-Crazy Test

At a certain young age we all hate the opposite sex. During this time, it is a huge insult to be accused of liking a member of the opposite sex, much less being "crazy" about a potential love interest. Grab the back of your male sibling's neck and tickle. If he bends his head back it means he is "girl crazy." On a girl, tickle her under the chin. If she leans her head forward, then she is "boy crazy." For shame.

Invisible

Pretend that your kid sibling is invisible and scan the room looking for him or her. This will inevitably cause the plainly visible child to giggle hysterically. After this quick scanning period is over, you are free to neglect the "invisible" kid for the next few hours and she will love every minute of it—a clear win-win situation for all.

Laugh It Off

Small children tend to fall down a lot. (It's okay, they're close to the ground.) Luckily for us, a little-known half second exists between an injury and loud wailing. During this time, a kid sibling will look around to see how to react. If you show any sympathy or compassion, prepare for waterworks. Instead, laugh uproariously. Unsure of what to do, your confused, mildly hurt sibling will probably choose to half smile just like Grandpa does when he didn't really hear what you said.

Stair Walk

It is often necessary to distract small siblings with laughter so that we can torture them later or escape punishment for recently delivered torture. In that case, the stair walk is an easily employed maneuver. Put a waist-high piece of furniture between you and your little sibling so that he can only see the top half of your body. Tell him you'll be taking the stairs, turn to one side,

and stomp jerkily while crouching a little bit at a time. Keep going until your head disappears. Now come back up the "stairs" the same way. Easily amused children will giggle and clap until their pudgy palms bleed.

Variation:
The Elevator

Similar in nature to the *stair walk*, this move requires pushing a button in the air and then smoothly bending the knees to give the appearance that you are descending in an elevator. Use this as an encore to the *stair walk*, as it's more boring to watch and harder to pull off.

Strong Ignore

The ultimate psychological move for use against kid siblings (and anybody else) also has a Zen-like simplicity—the strong ignore. No matter what happens, do not react to anything the attacker says or does. No matter how angry you become, show no emotion. Eventually, your sibling will simply get bored of messing with you. Holding out long enough to break this boredom barrier is the sign of a true Bro-master.

Tickle

A perfect combination of aggressive physical torture and acceptable social bonding, tickling is especially satisfying when the younger sibling is too small to escape. Concentrate soft finger jabs under the arms, along the rib cage, and to the tops of the thighs.

Variation:
The Tickle Worm

Wiggle your index finger threateningly, as though it were a small, angry worm. Now employ it for maximum torture. Use a *wrist grab* to pin your sibling's hands up high, exposing the sensitive armpits or belly. Now let her have it with the tickle worm.

Caution: May cause spontaneous urination.

Walkin' on the Moon

Want to throw your kid brother around the room but don't want to listen to him cry? Grab your little sibling under the arms and lift slightly, so his feet are barely touching the ground. This simulates the roughly one-third gravity that exists on the moon. When your sibling bends his knees and jumps, yank his limp little body as high as you can in the air.

Caution: Try to avoid ceiling fans and doorways, but know that the life of a child-astronaut is a life of danger.

Variation:
Walking on the Ceiling

For the tiniest of siblings, it is possible to go even further than *walkin' on the moon* and to warp the very fabric of their physical universe by reversing gravity. Grab the little sibling by the calves and lift so that she is hanging upside down. Now place her little feet on the ceiling and let her walk around. When she is older, she'll wonder how many of her childhood memories were really dreams.

Caution: Do not perform this move just after mealtime—unless you want to take a puke shower.

CONCLUSION

There are approximately five billion students of Bro-Jitsu alive in the world today (besides you). The style of this martial art may differ slightly in various regions of the world, but the core moves of Bro-Jitsu have remained unchanged for millennia: running after your siblings, running away from them, and telling on each other. Mastering Bro-Jitsu skills is a key part of growing up; it helps us figure out our own physical and mental limitations and how far to push the limits of others. Diligent Bro-Jitsu training pays off: children who follow the path of Bro-Jitsu are more aware of their surroundings; better tuned in to others' feelings; and well-prepared to excel in school, in the workplace, or in a no-holds-barred cage match.

But Bro-Jitsu doesn't end with childhood. Scientists have shown conclusively that many siblings will eventually grow up to become parents themselves. Although children may find this trend deeply disturbing, it must be noted that a well-trained student of Bro-Jitsu gains valuable insight and a considerable advantage when the time comes to fulfill the role of parental referee. Only an experienced Bro-master will be able to push his or her children to the pinnacle of Bro-Jitsu mastery; they will see through poorly delivered fibs; catch sloppy, behind-the-back goads; and deftly separate lazy squeals from real cries for help.

As adults, students of Bro-Jitsu are encouraged to join in conversation with their siblings at family gatherings to recount particularly clever, annoying, or profound Bro-Jitsu moves or situations. Reliving these memories serves both to strengthen family bonds and to hone future attacks and defenses. Remember: you are never too old to Bro-Jitsu.

Over the course of this book you have gained intimate access to dozens of shrewd maneuvers, their variations, and the crucial countermoves employed in the martial art of sibling rivalry. In addition, you have been shown the code of Bro-Jitsu. The paradoxical nature of this martial art can be difficult to grasp: a Bro-Jitsu encounter may switch from a dogged fight to the death to a tickling contest at a moment's notice. Bro-Jitsu is at once a martial art practiced by billions and an intensely personal family interaction. In your future campaigns, use these moves wisely and always honor the sacred vow of Bro-Jitsu.

Good luck walking the path of Bro-Jitsu. If you happen to discover new moves, variations, or countermoves, please share them with the Bro-Jitsu community at www.brojitsu.com.

INDEX

ACKNOWLEDGMENTS

Thanks go first and foremost to my wonderful family, for ensuring that my upbringing included heaping helpings of Bro-Jitsu. Thanks to my dad for helping me "walk on the ceiling" as a child, my mom for tickling me to the verge of vomiting, my aunts and uncles for humoring me (and a certain aunt and uncle for all the mean tricks—you know who you are), and my grandparents for serving dutifully as mostly immobile "home bases."

Extra special thanks go to my little brother. Every kidney punch I delivered was my way of saying, "I love ya, buddy." (And I look forward to telling you again this Thanksgiving.)

To my younger cousins, I must issue an apology and reiterate that forcing you to lick the shag carpet at grandma's house was all a part of your training, and nothing personal.

Heartfelt thanks to Dan Stern, etymologist extraordinaire.

As always, my gratitude goes to the people who

make books happen: my agent, Laurie Fox; my manager, Justin Manask; and my editors at Bloomsbury, Melanie Cecka and Margaret Miller. Thanks also to my illustrator, Les McClaine, who made the savage gauntlet of childhood come alive in these pages. (Check out the bug eyes on the looming girl on page 105 and tell me Les isn't a genius.)

And, of course, my heartfelt thanks go out to all of my friends and acquaintances who shared their stories of childhood battles. Every single person I spoke to had a fascinating and personal viewpoint on growing up with brothers and sisters. I feel privileged to have been given front-row seats to witness the triumphs and tragedies of those childhoods. I only hope that the lung- and soul-crushing moves in this book adequately convey the deep and sacred bonds described to me.

Finally, I must acknowledge the mountain of gratitude that I owe to a certain special someone, as she and I march bravely together into the wondrous realm of parental refereeing.

ABOUT THE AUTHOR

Daniel H. Wilson became an older brother at the age of two. Wilson began his Bro-Jitsu career with a promising early mastery of offensive moves, sadly rendered useless by a younger brother who quickly outgrew him. Adapting, Wilson employed the psychological aspects of Bro-Jitsu to maintain superiority based on a projected image of insanity and ruthlessness. Currently, Wilson focuses on honing his defensive maneuvers at annual Thanksgiving dinners and other family events held in his hometown of Tulsa, Oklahoma.

In addition to being a master of Bro-Jitsu, Daniel H. Wilson holds a PhD in robotics, and is the author of *How to Survive a Robot Uprising*, *Where's My Jetpack?*, and *How to Build a Robot Army*. He lives in Portland, Oregon.

www.danielhwilson.com
www.brojitsu.com

Note: In this image, Wilson employs a classic hair pull *maneuver* while his unlucky little brother issues a squeal, *presumably to the jaded parental referee holding the camera.*